CHRIST'S
LOVE
WILL
MAKE
YOU
LIVE

CHRIST'S LOVE WILL MAKE YOU LIVE

Walter Riess

Publishing House
St. Louis London

Concordia Publishing House, St. Louis, Missouri
Concordia Publishing House Ltd., London E. C. 1
Copyright © 1962, 1973 Concordia Publishing House

Library of Congress Catalog Card No. 72-97345
ISBN 0-570-03156-7

MANUFACTURED IN THE UNITED STATES OF AMERICA

For Mary Lois

CONTENTS

Photographs

Greer Cavagnaro — 8, 40, 48, 68
Wallowitch — 13, 60, 77
Bob Combs — 23, 26, 29, 44, 51, 57, 72, 81, 84

For You, Because He's Real

My blessing has been to know a lot of Christian young persons like you. To me these high school Christians are all wonderfully real people in Jesus Christ. I could never think of them in any other way.

But I can't help noticing that Christian teenagers *do not usually see themselves as wonderful people, or even worthy people*. They tend to run themselves down — in spite of all that God has done for them and in them. They often feel without meaning or purpose or attractiveness.

They find it hard to believe they are loved.

It's easy to understand why. The climaxes of adolescence we go through hurl to the surface of the mind the worst self-accusations. For the first time in life we stand alone, all alone, against all these accusations. Even our Christian faith can seem jittery and weak to us then.

This sense of loneliness and worthlessness attacks everyone. At your stage in life you know it well. What can help you?

Only this: remembering your place in the love of God, seeing how much He really does love you, seeing yourself as He sees you!

There are no other experiences that can equal this. Maybe you know it already. Maybe you're still to find it out for yourself. But — it's true.

Through books and high school discussion guides I have had the joy of putting to paper this Gospel love for youths. Almost every week I see how much the all-surrounding, all-enlivening love of Jesus Christ can mean to those who long to feel themselves wanted, loved, accepted, forgiven, and rejoiced over in heaven.

I have seen how much young persons ache to have their lives stand for something — especially in the times we have to live through and in the face of terrors that threaten to choke out the life and spirit of youth.

So, let His love try to reach some of these needs and wants which you feel — and which all of us must feel.

We can think together about this amazing offering of Himself, our Lord to us. We can remind each other that He is and that He is ours. We can meet each other in the warmth of His certain care.

God Loves You — Even at Your Worst

He loves you so much that He would die for you — for you alone.

He would die for you if you were the only person left on this earth.

His love means so much that nothing in life can mean much at all without it.

His love means you can feel what it is to be alive. His love means you can know deep in yourself what it is to be completely forgiven. What it is to be altogether wanted.

What it is to be wanted by God Himself just at that moment when you can't even want yourself. When you are most unlikable. Most unlovable. Most hateful even to you.

This is when God's love comes through sharpest and best. Just when you've given up on yourself. Just then.

Is it now?

How do you feel about yourself — right now?

Or do you always feel yourself a failure?

Listen to me. You may even *be* a failure — so far as people are concerned: the people in your high school or your home or even your church.

But how do you think you look to the God who

died for you? The God who watched His Son die for you?

To Him you cannot look like a failure.

Not after that.

To Him you *must* look like some treasure on the bottom of the ocean. You may have your weaknesses, but they are all covered over and washed by an ocean of shimmering love.

To Him you look like the whole reason for His living. Now that He has died for you, now that He has risen for you, now that He has spent Himself altogether for you — how else can He see you but as the full reason for His very being?

He is altogether set apart for you.

That's what "holy" means — wholly, wholly yours.

Think of how He sees you because of Jesus Christ.

Try seeing yourself through *this* ocean of love

And when you *can't* see yourself that way, no matter how hard you try, remember that He can't see you any *other* way.

For Jesus Christ is the way God is.

No matter where you are, right now.

In Spite of Yourself

You have your own place in His heart.

The Word of God's love always has to come to us *in spite* of — simply because there's always so much inside us that isn't for God at all.

13

In the high school years we know this without anyone telling it to us. We can't help feeling the tug and pull and jar of all the emotions filling us up right to the collar. We can't help looking at other people in high school and looking at them with so many crowding feelings.

Those feelings would fill a five-year diary. The jealousy in our own selves would pack a year of pages. How about the lust for the dreamboat? How about the hate for the person who's got everything — who's got it made 100%? And then the stacked-up and completely *mixed*-up messes of love and hate and longing and resenting we breed in ourselves whenever we get into it with our parents!

You may think you're a new model when you sense this stuff of anguish piling up inside you. But you aren't even a recent model. You're just exactly what all of us have been since the Garden of Eden started us off on our journey of discovery.

We carry our worst enemies right around inside us, and we know it. And quite often we get afraid about it — afraid that no one, *not even Jesus Christ,* could possibly love us.

That's when the worst happens to us.

When we start seeing ourselves *only* as we look to ourselves.

When we start living on this one level only — and ignore the level on which God stands.

14

When we live from inside out instead of from outside in.

For the truth is that when we are most unlovable, God can show His mercy and grace to us the best.

While we were yet sinners, He died for us! — That's New Testament.

Herein is love, not that we loved Him but that He loved us! That's New Testament too.

Bringing it squarely to you: When you are yet a sinner, He dies for you. He rises again for you. He lives right now for you.

It is the way He is that counts, not the way you are.

It is the way He loves that adds up to your whole world and your whole breath.

He loves enough even to cover you.

I know. Because His love is enough to cover even me.

Your Church Is Your Personal Home

I know this from my own experience in the ministry. I knew it from the start of my preaching, when I would sit for long hours in the office of my own church in Detroit. There were the warm walls that surrounded the prayers spoken in the depths before Sunday's worship. There were the late afternoon pages, written after a call on some tired and ailing parishioner.

I knew it through those evenings when young people would come into the setting of red curtains and Walnut paneling to talk about entering the holy ministry, or just to say what was in their hearts about their future marriage or their job or their school. I knew it that very late evening when one of these young people knelt with me at the altar, still and alone in the towering chancel. In that moment we both realized with a perfect, white clearness what a home to our spirits our church could be.

Then the worship itself — the soaring, rising, singing praise of a whole people. The organ chorale, the sacrament, the thinking together that we did in the sermon. And all the while that same quiet surrounding of our church, that same almost unearthly peace and stillness.

Then, sometimes, our special youth vespers, held late at night after some meeting. The solemn re-dedication of lives, the longing for the Lord Jesus Christ, the gradual or sudden dawning of a new fantastic light on souls that had never before dreamed that such a brightness could be born within themselves.

I remember that first church office, that first church with such joy only because I came to know in living touch the living meaning of the *church*.

It is a meaning I like to talk about with young persons who are looking for the true meaning of their lives. It is an experience that I cannot help talking about with people like you.

Today more than ever before we can share these overwhelming blessings with each other. For our times have grown even more restless and insecure. Our futures have moved deep into shadow. And the actual truth is that there is no home at all left for our personalities but the home that is our church!

Can you point to your high school as that home? Your future job? Your dream of a life with your life's partner? Can you think of any of these things as your real home when our world may shatter about us at any moment? Can you hold to popularity or status in your group when a global crisis can change everything in a week's time?

Where's your insurance policy for all this?

"The world has come of age," wrote a martyred

German pastor looking at the ruin around him. Whatever security the world used to offer has long since gone down the drain. All of us — youth *and* adults — feel the tragic ache of a loneliness and a hunger for the sure and the certain.

I believe that the sure and the certain is there. I know it is there for you and for me.

That is what I want to write about — *you,* and *the certainty that your Lord Jesus Christ offers you in His church today,* right now, as never before.

Sometimes, in fact I think this is why our Lord has let so much of our world crumble around us. He has a reason beyond our imagining.

He wants us to see as never before the love of Himself offered for us, the love of His people now handed to us, and the real peace of soul that is there for us — all in the surrounding warmth of His church. All in the abiding peace of His sanctuary, His presence in these human walls.

Because there is no other place to look, we must look here as if our lives depended on it.

They do.

The only question — the last question — is *how.*

How do we look? *How* can this church of ours become a surrounding home to our spirits? *How* will our Lord lead us into a shining relationship with our own people — His people?

How can we discover this place to be home?

The answer is out of this world. It is your gift from Jesus Christ Himself. For He called the church His body. And He will not leave His followers to search hopelessly for His own body, His own presence, in a day like ours.

So share our church with me. Admit that you long for your real home. Look carefully how to build that home around your life. See closely how the blessing of that home can fill you inside and out with a richness and a quiet joy.

Remember, it *is* all there. It *is* real. And it *is* for you.

There's No Time Like Right Now

Right now you are growing at a rate that you will never equal again the rest of your life — growing not just in body but in mind. Your personality is taking shape just as the muscles and limbs of your body are reaching for maturity.

You have an emotional sensitivity to your faith and its meaning that will quite possibly never reach this peak again. Nobody knows exactly why you can experience such an intense joy and richness when you come into a living meeting with your church. But this much is true: It can happen. It does happen.

I have seen it happen in countless young Christian lives. I remember it happening in my own high school life. At no time before did the full impact of my Lord and my church move me as during adolescence. And time and again I have read in the biographies of Christians how wonderfully and miraculously the meaning of their faith came home in these years.

Of course the same sensitivity that opens us so completely to the joys of our faith can open us to the pain and struggle of growing up. The one almost always goes with the other. If this is the time in your life when you can see into the meaning of your Lord and your church better than any other, it is also the time when you will feel the hurt of really liking someone who does not like you. It is the time when you will learn you have some terrifying limitations as well as some unexpected talents.

I think our Lord made us this way — to have this one time in our lives when we feel more deeply than ever before or ever again. Nothing proves more His love for you than that He Himself is prying open your soul so that His life may flood into your life. So that He may own you and hold you in an awareness of His everlasting presence!

Even Christian teens wonder out loud how close their Lord can seem to them at some times — and how far away at others! But what no girl or boy *can* realize is how far away God can seem *after* the high school years — especially if these most precious adolescent years are not put to their high spiritual use.

It is too late, after the high school years, to recapture the mood, the desire, the chemical balance, the sensitivity of these days in your life. The emotions you are feeling right now will always seem something special to you. And they should. For nothing like them will happen to you again this side of eternity. Right now — right now — God is holding Himself out to you in a driving, loving, vibrant outreach.

This is what you are feeling. This is the truth you sometimes know better than anything else.

True, all of your life God will be reaching out for you. He won't — He *can't* — stop doing *that!*

But never again might you be so conscious of it.

These are the years when falling in love comes easily.

These are the years when falling in love with your Lord can fill your whole life with one meaning, one joy, one steady goal.

There just is no life without it — no life at all.

Your Inner Feelings Are Saying Something

Most likely our Lord gives you more *awareness* of Him right now than earlier or later in your life.

It's also possible that even now feelings run up and down inside you — not steady like a jet stream, but bobbing like a raft on an ocean.

That's the way we are built, from the ground of youth on.

And that's why, for one reason, we need our church the way lungs need air.

We simply have to connect our inner spiritual life with a place, a group of people — a home where we don't have to *feel* the presence of God to *know* He is with us and for us and always ours.

Picture your church as a gift of God that puts into solid, touchable shape all of His other gifts to you.

Do you want to see the love of Jesus Christ? Look at the real, touchable crucifix in your chancel. Or see the painting that puts Him before your eyes in one or the other scene of His life, death, or resurrection.

Do you want to see for yourself the history of His people and their praises to Him? Pick up your church hymnal and leaf through it, reading a verse here and there that seems to speak to you particularly.

Do you hunger for visible, touchable evidence that God loves you and will keep you in His care? Touch the wafer of bread and taste the wine that carries into your very body His own body and blood! Or walk up to the baptismal font, and remember how once *you* were brought there — and how you will carry that Baptism with you ever single day of your life.

All this is the grace of Jesus Christ coming to you personally in wood and stone and cloth and paper and bread and wine — and even water. It is God taking your feelings and kneading them right into the boards and the bricks of your church building and then placing you there to make sure you're constantly refreshed with all of it.

Really, then, when you look deep into your church, you look deep into God Himself, into God's people, and even into yourself. You see the whole history of His love for you. You see your friends taking that love and radiating it out among themselves and into your life too. And you see all of this in the realness of cross and font and Communion cup — and in the miracle of the Word of God moving through pulpit and sacraments into your flesh and blood.

What more could you ask of any place or of anything in our kind of a world?

God Reaches You —
Even When You Don't Want Him To

Sometimes He reaches you at the most uncomfortable times.

You catch yourself telling a dirty story. Or despising a sermon with a snigger. Or thinking of *you* — like a cracked record on a turntable — in every situation you face through the day.

Suddenly a warning light starts blinking inside your brain. Wait a minute — you aren't even *acting* like a Christian, like God's person. How do you look to people around you who are using you as a mirror for God, for God's church, for God's love? What's happened here, inside you, outside you, to make you so much *un*like who you really are?

It's pain. It's no good. Guilt feelings! Shiver down the spine like a razor blade. Take a shower. See a show. It'll go away.

What will go away? The guilt feelings? Sure.

And maybe our self, running right down the drain of self-satisfaction. Our personalities bathing themselves in a soft, yellow light of see-nothing, hear-nothing, tell-nothing about self. Our personalities running away as fast as sleds downhill on ice.

Our selves running away from *God*.

Because that's what is happening when we drive off from our selves our knowing of the good from the bad, the right from the wrong. When just automatically we duck feelings that tell us we have not been living His life through the drive and power of the love of Jesus Christ!

Our Lord does not just let us flout His way, His will — and to leave us skidding down our hills without a word from Him. If He were to treat us this way for long, we'd all be so far from Him by now that we wouldn't even know His name.

He reaches us. He reaches us with His Law —

His will working its power in us. He reaches us with His Gospel — His love powering our lives like some gigantic waterfall powering a generator, lighting a city, driving the machines that keep a city living

He reaches us because He is all for us.

He reaches us because He is love even when we are anything but love ourselves.

He reaches us because He is outreach, because He is longing, because He *is* compassion for high school years and high school yearnings.

Because He really is always altogether with us.

The Light of Happiness

Happiness that now and then flashes up in us can leave the rest of our lives looking pretty drab to us. Like a high school job we face after a week at the lake, or like the kitchen after a wedding party.

Faith has its unhappy victories and its long, long

moments after the storms of light. At least this is the way the battle looks to us, especially at the start of it. Often, in fact, our big delights — our highest and clearest and purest moments in faith — come to us before a letdown. And we may spend the rest of our lives wondering what's wrong with us that our happiness in Jesus Christ is no brighter.

This is a far from uncommon complaint. To a good many Christian young persons it is a complaint accompanied by painful self-blame. Somehow we get to feel that Christian joy must radiate on our faces like a Pepsodent smile, or it isn't there. We have to carry our souls beaming like a flashlight, or our souls are dying.

This is the kind of smile-and-the-world-smiles-with-you imagining that some have parlayed into a million-dollar business. People like to buy Bibles guaranteed to bring peace of mind under "Chosen Texts with Positive Appeal." People like to hire preachers who can "portray life with power" Sunday after Sunday and never let on that the world has sunk as low as it seems to have sunk.

Worse still, people like to take Christ off the cross and turn Him into a Galilean psychiatrist, uttering smiley words of personality-plus from the "other side" of Calvary.

The trouble is that Jesus Christ Himself never gave any backing to "popular appeal" stuff. The Man who sweat blood in Gethsemane could hardly do it without making a lie of His whole life and death and resurrection. The Man who sent His closest friends out to certain death — just for talking about Him — could not want to be the force behind the Pepsodent smile in any pulpit.

Nor could He be the real reason for our feelings if we do not glimmer with public relations glow at every turn of our daily road. Although I think Jesus Christ may have smiled once in a while, and probably did, I cannot see that He smiled all of the time. And I can't see why we must feel that being one of His followers demands something that He Himself did not accent at all!

Jesus Christ knew what life was all about — more than we know. He knew what high school life is all about. He knew that life had an end higher than itself. It is easy to preach "Positive Appeal for Daily Living" if daily living forms the be-all and end-all of existence. But if daily living becomes that important, I doubt that even an angel in heaven could bring happiness — the kind of Christian joy we're going to be talking about — into it.

Jesus Christ knew much better.

To Him life always meant life with God, life completely shaped *above* oneself, life nurtured and fed and molded and tenderly and eternally touched by God. Life meant a different kind of breath than *just* breathing, than *only* living, than *only* clawing our way from morning to morning dry and broken inside like old twigs in winter, our spirits longing only to see another day and another popularity contest which we can never really win.

Life meant Himself in us.

Life meant Himself in us *in spite* of anxiety, in spite of all the clawing, in spite of all the very hard and very real living we have to do just to build our lives. The life of God does not cancel out the pressures of daily living. But that life does go on far underneath all those pressures, like a river running under and through and around the great rooms of a cave. The cave is there — and the horribly frightening echoes and pockets of fear and darkness of wonder. But life is there too. Life, and so light.

Because God has set His ground in us. He has lighted a stretch of His own land in us. And this — nothing less — is happiness.

Joy is to know this even when we cannot see it — even when it is not right to boast about it. Joy is to believe that we have Him, a part of us even when there is absolutely nothing on earth or on our faces to help us prove it to others. Joy is to know this when every single human reason for it is ripped away, at a time when we have to tear away from the crowd or from a pet love or a pet hate. Or in the tumbling of our hopes and ambitions around the wreck of our education. Or in the hours of unexplained pain in some dark hospital room.

Joy is where He is, no matter what.

The Glamor Myth Versus You

We live right in the middle of the loudest mental bombardment ever inflicted on a people. Our television sets, our radios, our newsstands, our billboards, our advertisements, our magazines, and the All-American Hollywood Jungle Gym pour out on us at an absolutely ridiculous rate a mountain of words and pictures.

All of these words and pictures have one purpose, one goal.

The goal is you. To make you a "glamor" person.

The goal is to give you an idea of what life is all about — your life — or at least what it *should* be all about.

This is the Gospel According to the Communications Industry.

It is the gospel according to the liquor ads and the girlie magazines and the auto showrooms.

It is a gospel that his clicked too. It has won every city in America and a good many in Europe too. It runs our beauty pageants, our Academy Awards, and writes our ads. It runs Hollywood, the New York TV cameras, and writes copy to "sell" every budding starlet from Dubuque to Seattle.

Just why is it the number-one glamor-sell power in our country? If you could answer this, you'd see in an instant the greatest gaping hole in our "way of life." You'd spot it in plain daylight — the lie of the American glamor myth

The lie says: "If you have it, you have happiness. If you don't have it (the car, the ranch home, the status paycheck, the store-window wife, the high-ranking, high-climbing hubby), you can't get happiness on a bet."

What's wrong with it? Isn't it true, or most of it? Or would you like to live out of a tin plate, ride a horse to a job in the ditches, and scrounge a living from a two-year education?

Most of us don't want to live like that. But does that mean we could never be happy if we *had* to live like that! One thing is sure — we can be a lot happier living like that than we can ever be living by the Great Lie.

The trouble with the glamor myth is that it makes an idol out of a living standard. And idolatry in any form is just another word for misery. You start worshiping something besides God, and inwardly you know that your worship is killing off your first love. You feel this happening in yourself — but by then it may be too late to find your way back out of your idolatry.

For a time you try to live it out, live it up, make it work. You trade in status symbols like a native trades in beads. You go along with the high school crowd no matter where the crowd is headed — if anywhere. You live out the lies of your outfit no matter what, no matter where, no matter why. That's one thing you can never stop to ask — why?

How could you ask it? There isn't an answer around. Not for selling your soul to a fake dream. Not for making a god out of a way-of-life jag, even if that jag has a whole nation's movie industry for a sponsor.

Don't believe it. No one's your friend who sells you a lie.

Your Friend is the one who says: "Blessed are the poor in spirit" — and then comes into you to live *that* out with you.

Over the Long Run

Nothing much ever happened, besides Jesus Christ that can fill a person with joy over the long run of days and nights. But even so — even when we have His life alive in us and even when we feed that life with the Gospel — the signs of joy that come from our eyes and our lips are few and far between.

That's all right. God did not command Christian teens to be grinning with happiness from dawn to dusk. The reasons for *not* grinning could make a book for any one of us to write, provided we had enough paper on hand to cover the subject. They are reasons found in the overall confusion, frustration, effort, and uncertainties of living.

But the prime reason for us not to expect a carnival life is God Himself. "Take up your cross and follow Me," He said, and He wasn't headed for an amusement park. "Three times I asked the Lord to remove this thorn from me!" Paul wrote, still in pain, "But He said, 'My grace is enough for you.' "

Not only enough for you, he might have added, but for all that happens to you. And if you are a Christian, not all that happens to you will have the smell of a new car about it.

Yet the strangest truth of all starts to dawn on us when we discover how the apostle lived quite happily and productively *in spite of his personal tragedies*. Whatever it was that crippled him, that mired him down into pain, he managed to write more classic thank-yous, both to his Lord and to his people, than we could count in one reading.

Most of these thank-yous, in fact, are hidden in places where you miss them at first glance. They pop up in the most unlikely spots. So often Paul links them with things that to us sound utterly repulsive. Yet — "I will glory in my infirmities." *I will be happy because of my weaknesses!*

At this point you reach the miraculous. The miracle of joy in suffering. There's nothing like it in the Christian faith except the miracle of the resurrection itself, the resurrection of the body to glory on the Last Day. But this — the possibility of *rejoicing* in the worst agony that can threaten us, the lowest feelings that can drag at our heels — this is all sheer miracle of Jesus Christ.

It is to my thinking the one surest sign of His presence with us on earth. To say that this rejoicing in the worst of pains is possible sounds impossible. But to know it through living is possible. Some Christian sufferers have startled themselves learning it.

Even surgeons and physicians have told of this mystery. They say that some people of faith find more joy through their suffering than they had known before it. These sufferers are not addicts to the doctor's office, either. They are people who have been driven to hospital beds and to home confinement by the real torments that afflict all of us at one time or another in our lives — even in the high school years.

I have a private theory about all this. It may be valid, or it may not. Certainly it is true that Jesus Christ Himself did a tremendous lot of suffering in His earthly stay, even if that stay lasted only 33 years. And perhaps when we suffer, really suffer, we come to understand Him better — not just His suffering but His immense heart, His pity, His infinite care that transcends even the agony that aspirin cannot reach.

Not that aspirin doesn't help. Medicine belongs to God's healing providence as much as anything else, I suppose, including the scalpel. But no medicine can deaden human suffering endlessly. Even the most powerful drug wears off in its effects — and leaves man a stumbling, dark-ridden, suffering human being.

Only the torrential sympathy, "suffering with," of Jesus Christ can match both this suffering and the darkness that always approaches with it. There is more than a match in Him for it all. Just as the crown of thorns He wore before His crucifixion has become a victory before men, so can the most intense Christian suffering lead us into those gleaming conquests of faith otherwise beyond experience.

"Take up your cross and follow Me," He said. Well?

God in Your Love Life

He often seems as hidden and deep a mystery as the whereabouts of the light switch in a darkroom. We muddle along, first this guy, then the next — first this girl, then another — and at last we say, "I'm in love!" Then we go steady for a week or a year, break up, start all over again, hitch our wagon to another star, fall in love, fall out of love.

Someday out of all this we may find a marriage partner. We may even be happy with that marriage. But we may also be just plain miserable. Then we scowl back on these years. *What went wrong? What was I looking for, anyway?*

Chances are you're looking for a lot of things in any person you like. Romance. Fun. Companionship. The works. And every time you go out, you hold this person up to an inside measuring stick and ask, "What's for me?"

You're playing the wrong game.

You're asking, "What can this person *give me?*" You might be asking, "What can *I give this person?*"

The one you're going with has a life with God (I hope). So do you. When you go out together, you first of all want to make sure that you *build up* this life of God in each other.

In other words, you don't want just a good time. You want to make this night — this *event* — count for a plus in God's plan for His people.

That doesn't mean necessarily "talkin' religion." But it certainly does mean talking and acting as *God's person*. And if you act as God's person, a channel carrying the love of God in Jesus Christ through to another person, you aren't going to live in passion pit. You aren't going to paw over each other until the only thing you can think of is yourself, your need. You aren't going to draw yourself off-key with cheap jokes.

All these don't make very pretty ways for being and acting as Christ's person with another Christian. But look at your chance! Look at your chance to treat love, and emotion, and desire even, and touch, and boy-with-girl as one who has God first in life, and God's life first inside!

Think of how a boy feels toward a girl when he sees that God has taken over her life — when he can tell that from being with her. Think how a Christian girl feels toward a boy whose every treatment of her says: "I'm out to build up *your* life with God — and nothing I do will ever injure your life with Him, or mine"

Actually, God is putting a person right within your reach. Precious few opportunities can rival this one — its closeness, its deep meanings for the future, its chance for really sharing the most vital loves of our life.

How does all this help you?

Well, if you can't think of a friend in this light, ask yourself why you're going together? Why this person and not another? Why *can't* you see yourself as God's person with this friend? Why do you *have* to act as if you're living only for flesh thrills with that other date? If you simply cannot share any vital loves of your life together, what's blocking off the current?

Above all, ask yourself how you could carry God's life into a marriage with a person you can't talk with, even about faith! For this is the real job of marriage, loving each other as Christ loved the church, building each other in Him, strengthening each other's calling in Him, talking life to each other.

That immense job has to start now. If it doesn't start now, when will it?

Think it over — before the next chapter in your love life.

What's Wrong, and What Isn't?

A group of eleven high school girls in Illinois asked the question.

They had taken a poll among themselves and found that each girl differed from every other member of the group when they tried to pinpoint what was wrong, and what not wrong, about some things they were doing socially.

All this difference of opinion raised a much bigger question. If Christian girls couldn't agree on the bad or the good in social habits, how could anyone else agree on what was sin? And if no one could really agree — especially in girl-boy relating — what did it actually mean to talk about sin at all? Why bother with it?

The girls had reason to wonder. But they didn't have to bolt clear out of the picture of sin. It's simply never easy for anyone to paint blacks and whites. Life doesn't come packaged that way, in neat checkerboard squares with a winning game clearly marked with dotted lines.

Life comes packed with gray areas, light grays and dark grays, cloudy and milky and filled with details that don't always make sense.

Most of these gray areas start moving into focus

in the high school years. Before then, parents seem to have the answers — all of them. But not now. Not maybe ever again.

The gray areas seem to get grayer as life gets more social. One of the girls in this group of eleven felt that "necking" was definitely "sinful." Another felt that a Christian girl could neck a half hour with a boy and not have a "sinful" thought at all.

Who's right? Who's wrong?

Both can be right. Probably both were.

One girl revealed herself in responding, so did another. One girl said that necking stirred up *in her* thoughts that bothered her conscience. The other girl felt that necking did nothing of the sort — for her! And maybe it didn't.

For one girl an act was wrong. For another girl the same act was dangerous but perhaps not wrong.

Nothing gives us a black-and-white answer to the question of necking or embracing or casual show of affection between unmarrieds. In fact, the Bible answers very few questions black on white. Evidently God doesn't think life comes that way, either.

What God wants is that we grow into such a relationship *to Him* that we can accept the grays in courage and faith. In the name of Jesus Christ and through the power of the Holy Spirit we can have such a growing life — such a throbbing, pulsing life that we can meet these gray areas *in terms of our own personal relationship to God.*

It takes life to live life. It takes a lot of life inside us to meet the whole glob of life that goes on outside us.

What you want to watch in yourself is not that you keep a notebook padded with "all the answers." It might prove to be a pretty thin notebook after all. But what you do want is to keep that still, deepest center of your *self* completely apart for Him — altogether *for* Him.

You want to know that no matter how many gray areas you have to wade through outside, you have this clear, clean innner center of your self to which you can retreat. A place for you to go, far inside yourself, any time, no matter what your doubt or wonder or fear.

Think now a minute. Probe to the very deepest part of you. What do you hear? What do you see?

When everything nonessential is subtracted from you, layer by layer, what stays? What stands strong and sure?

Do you find God's love there, in that inner center — in that core of yourself?

Don't Give Up on Yourself

No one gets off pain-free from mistakes. Not even you. Not even St. Paul. *He* called himself "the worst of sinners."

A Midwest girl writes that she has ruined her boyfriend's life by giving in to his desires. She blames herself for letting her emotions carry her out of bounds. She says: "Now no matter what I do or how I change, I'll always know I destroyed another person, his education, his chances for life."

Well, I could say something. But I won't.

What she's destroyed — or never had to start with — is an honest Christian idea of the risks a person has to take in living. You can't live without blundering. And since living involves other people besides yourself, you can't live without blundering into their lives too.

Not that our girl did right in letting a boy have his way with her. Not at all. Too bad she can't call it back, all of it. But now that she has made her aching blunder, she *could* remind herself that *she* is the reason why Jesus Christ lived and loved and died and rose again.

It's exactly this reminding yourself — every morning — that *all* of God is yours that makes life life. Without this reminding going on, you're at the mercy of every hideous mistake that human flesh and bones can fall into. That's no fun — to be at the mercy of yourself. That's funlessness itself. That's a living death.

Therefore it's anything but Christian to be constantly knocking yourself down and out for being "such a terrible sinner." If you spend all your days

49

thinking this way, it will get you right back exactly where you started. For you are stuck not only on your blunders but on yourself. You are saying: "Look at *me,* how bad I am — how lousy!"

What you want to say is: "Look at *Him!*"

Even when you do feel miserable about yourself, you aren't going to break out of that misery by burying yourself in it. That's simply not your business as a Christian personality. Your business is to live *Him,* to reflect *Him,* to pass on *His life* to anyone around you who needs life.

That's why your worst moments can be your best. They can be, that is, *if* you master that crucial art of reminding yourself that God is spending Himself for you in His Son. When you do this self-reminding strongest, you carry life to others strongest. You breathe the Spirit of God when you know in yourself how much you need that Spirit.

So if you feel you're about as poor an example of a Christian as you can be, welcome to the club.

But more than that, welcome to the club of the redeemed, the bought-back ones.

The living ones.

Not Just a Knock on the Door

Not "Somebody up there" or "the all-seeing All" or the "Great Beyond" or whatever else the song-scribblers manage to squeeze into the lines.

None of this is God.

51

Nothing so much shows how poor we can become in our faith life than the red-tag labels we sometimes pin on God the Father, Son, and Holy Spirit. For labeling Him is like labeling the bottles in a cola plant. It's the last thing that happens before the bottles get shipped, forgotten, sold out.

Once you've captured your God with a slippery word, you don't have to take Him seriously any more. He's all wrapped up under your tongue — and so is the whole purpose and loving work of Jesus Christ and the whole re-creating life of the Holy Spirit.

God Himself means more to you than a "Friend up there." He who is working outside you and through you and in you every moment of your breath, He who drives and powers your life and your words, He who dies for you and lives for you and reigns for you — He cannot stand to be labeled. You might as well try to label the Niagara or tag the jungles of the Congo.

Or try to label His love for you. Try to label how He goes on loving you and loving you with the immense outpouring of His heart. Try to add up how the river-running mercy of His breast overwhelms your every single day with utter and complete forgiveness and kindness.

No young person can live without this. Not you. Not I. This love is our breathing. This love is our living.

Would you like to place an easy-to-read tag on your whole life? Or can't you?

The very fact that God is God makes a label out of the question. If you have such a god now, you ought to spell him with a small g. He isn't worth the words you're wrapping him in.

Our real God and Lord is unwrappable, untaggable, unlabelable, and altogether worth knowing with your whole self. Not just the great beyond but the great here-and-now. Not just the here-and-now but the forever. Not just the forever but the final. Always moving into and around our lives with the explosive force of His love, always guiding unseen, always ruling the world even through the people who deny Him, and in spite of them causing His will to be done on the earth.

Always loving you, cherishing you, caring for you, blessing you — even when you think He is miles from you. Even when you cannot feel Him near, and maybe especially then, His love is flowing around you like a rushing river.

When you are darkest, He is most light. When you are saddest, He is most hope. When you have given up on yourself, He comes swiftest and surest. When you cannot stand the sight of yourself in the mirror, He loves to see you and holds your face before His own with a tenderness you cannot imagine.

You He loves. *You* He longs for with an agony and a cry into your dark nights.

What does He call you?

He has no label for you. No price tag.

You cost Calvary.

There is no price to match Calvary. There is no price tag to match you.

You are something else.

Finding Love

Being loved is the secret behind how *to* love.
If you don't know that by now, you don't know
the full glory of being Christian. For every glory
we have, every beauty we prize, every shred of delight in being Christian flow out of this certainty
that God loves us to the end and beyond the end.

The hardest thing about this love — this being
loved — is that we can't always find a reason inside
ourselves *for* being loved. No matter what mirror
we pick up, we don't see much of a lovable character
in it — not unless we put on a false face somewhere.
Our own face we know too well to kid ourselves
about. We know what the face has done, what it is
capable of doing — even to our friends — and we
know what it has done to ourselves.

We get caught, then, between how we see ourselves (ouch!) and how God sees us. Somehow we
keep mixing up the two. The result is that we make
God as small as we are, or sometimes try to make
ourselves as big as God is.

God loves us — *but not because of us.* He loves
us because of Jesus Christ.

All this love comes from clear outside ourselves.
Love comes as a gift. It either comes that way

or it doesn't come at all. Love comes because God loves. Love comes because God's Son Jesus Christ loves. Love comes because *He* loves *us!*

Talk in a circle? Maybe.

Because love does form a circle. From our Lord, through us, out to people, and so back to Him again.

That's why finding love always means reminding yourself that *God* loves. It does *not* mean reminding yourself that you can love either God, yourself, or other people on your own power.

Your own power won't carry you far here. It's like ultra-cut-rate gas. When the hills loom up ahead, the gas starts sputtering out. When you find it hard even to like yourself, you need something more than your own power to go on living.

You need to be loved. You need to know it. You have to love it. You have to love it so much you spread it around.

The best thing of all is this: You can grow every single day of your life — in sensing His love around you, and in passing it on.

What else is Christian serving all about?

No Ifs and Buts in our Faith

A flyer friend of mine likes to cartoon the distress
of an amateur airlines pilot as he tries to tell his
passengers of their peril:

"Friends, this is your pilot speaking. Our altitude is 4,800 feet. Our air speed is 270 miles per hour. There are however a few difficulties at the present time. The terrain below seems slightly unfamiliar. In fact, we seem to be over water. There is a bit of a problem with the fuel. Apparently we are running somewhat low. Nothing to worry about, I assure you. Just a few items that your captain and co-pilot will be ironing out in the minutes ahead. . . ."

It's not really so funny to think of ourselves getting stuck with a pilot like that. But the amazing thing about us is that we make ourselves a pilot like that in our faith life. We hear the full, free Gospel of Jesus Christ, but it comes over our microphones like the hemming and hawing of a novice pilot. It comes over something like: "Friends, this is your Savior speaking. I would like to help you so much, really, but . . ."

There are always a lot of *buts* we can think of at any given moment in our bustle and scurry. We can think of more *buts* and *ifs* than psalms and hymns and spiritual songs any day, Sundays included.

Part of the trouble is that our age is so naturally full of question marks. There's no doubt of this, and I don't think we ought to play it down when we try to take a sharp look at how things really are with us.

But the question marks could not loom so hazardous, and our response to them could not be so filled with fear, if we were to possess a relationship with Jesus Christ as the number-one fact of our breathing. Living spirals into confusion only when everything we see and suspect draws equally on our attention. Think of yourself standing before a carnival ferris wheel at night, trying to follow with your eyes every single light — yellow, green, blue, red — that swims before your vision. What would happen? What dizziness, what indecision would rob you of any possible joy or amusement!

Something like this happens when we hear the Gospel or discuss it without letting it drill down into the center of our being. It becomes just one more perplexing item in a long scale of puzzlements, one more obstacle in an already jammed obstacle course. We see neither the Christ nor ourselves clearly. Instead we try to hold our vision to an already overwhelming swirl of colored lights, all of them as phony as the string of bulbs on a ferris wheel.

Jesus Christ is this way: He takes the center of our lives, or He adds to the already deep and sometimes terrifying pain of them. His Gospel of love and redeeming digs into the underpinnings of the soul. We need Him longingly and inwardly.

We can have Him too — minus the ifs and the buts.

The Biggest Problem of Your Life

You might find your own particular worst worry somewhere in this list, drawn up by a small Christian teen-age group:

1. Controlling my own emotions and desires.
2. Achieving independence without overrebelling against my parents and other adults.
3. Carrying over my faith into my high school life — learning how to apply what I believe to how I live.
4. Going with persons of other faiths.
5. Mastering my desires — especially in the area of sex.
6. Participating in my church and finding it meaningful enough to stay enthused about it.
7. Developing a really working relationship with Scripture.
8. Coming to a certain and sure communion with God in my everyday life.
9. Discovering how to keep from putting people and things before God in my life.
10. Knowing myself well enough to tell when I am in love — and when it is right for me to get married.

There were other problems, and they could be mentioned anywhere in the list. So could your particular constant pal — your tagalong worry or self-concern. If it isn't there already, you could put it into the list in boldface type, underlined. You probably know it that well by now.

You know it so well by now, you've lived with

it so long that you'd be happy to trade with any other person reading this chapter. The only trouble is that he or she might jump over a fence to trade with you.

You might end up worse than you started out. In fact, you might be so surprised to learn what a burden someone else has been carrying around that you'd never complain again.

Happy-go-lucky Fred's got everything — football uniform included (with name in box score and big *hero* label). Sunny Suzy struts around the field in the halftime, when Fred's in the locker room. She grins from mascara to mascara. The good Lord handed her life on a platter (including Fred). You'd love to be out there too, but you're waterlogged up in the stands — always the idolizing, never the idol.

What you don't know is the story of Fred's home life or Sunny Suzy's inner turmoil. Behind all the touchdowns and the baton twirls there's a lot of wrestling going on, a lot of wondering, a lot of the same kind of stuff you've waded through, only worse.

Some Christians manage to look like Suzy and Fred almost all the time. All the time you see them, anyway. Some of these Christians may try to convince you that just *being* in the church automatically solves all the problems — or should. If your problems aren't solved for you, then there's something wrong with your faith! You'd better take stock, sister and brother.

Well, go ahead and take stock all you want. But if all you find in yourself is a grin, *then* start worrying. Because then you really aren't meeting life at all. You're cheating yourself — and the people around you — by dodging the very real problems and crises that any real life places squarely in front of you.

Don't be ashamed to have problems and to admit it. But don't be ashamed, either, to admit you have a Lord God just a mile or two taller than the tallest problem you will ever face.

You can't know all the answers. You never will.

But you can know the One who has all the answers. Even the answers for *you*.

Your Personality Rises to the Gospel

This Gospel — the good news of Jesus Christ putting His life into us and around us through His own life and death and resurrection — strikes our personalities like a whirlwind strikes a millpond.

Suddenly the wind becomes alive again, the storm churns the pond into whitecaps and into unimaginable power. Stagnant, stale water spins into life, sprays out into the air and onto the shore. If you stand near that pond, you feel its spray.

It would be nice if you could take that storm and put it in your pocket — or if you could pen up the whirlwind under your own combination lock. But you can't do anything.

God is doing the doing.

Probably most attempts to cage the whirlwind of the Gospel come from inner doubts that God is really reaching out for us.

Here the problem leaps up with a threat in front of us. If we have never seen such a love before, never felt such a knocking at our heart before, how can we possibly know divine love when it comes to us? How can we handle it? What can we do with it?

The answer disturbs us no end. We *cannot* handle it. We cannot "know it" as we know human love.

We can only live on it.

We can only sense its power in us and around us. We and only know the force of the Gospel as we know the force of the light that streams from an electric bulb or as we sense the power of a waterfall from the white swirl of it that smashes to the rocks below. That is how we finally have to come to see our lives — in the frame of the seafoam sent into the atmosphere around us by the limitless power of God dashing on the rocks of our soul.

The Gospel of Jesus Christ is power itself. You can't stop it or trap it or take it apart, piece by piece, to see what makes it so. It simply *is* so. The Gospel alone can rush so penetratingly to the lowest reaches of our souls that everything — everything — seems mockery that tries to imitate it.

That's why Jesus Christ could act so harshly with the love for money. That's why He could deal so sharply with the rich young man who could not bear to separate himself from this pile of charm that seemed to be calling to *his* soul. That account held a lot of money — a lot of the great American goddess of *dollars*. (In this case it wasn't the goddess of sex or the two-, three-, four-, and five-ranking goddesses of status, success, education, and social position.)

Whatever it is that calls to the deepest part of

the Christian — if it isn't the Gospel, it's an idol. And the young person who falls for the sugary talk of the false yen is settling his life for the skim level, the top two inches, where nothing really ever happens.

But worst of all is to hold a double-level life. The worst is to know there flows a stream of joy somewhere within, and then to live as if it weren't there. To give yourself to every call that calls and to lose the one call that counts — this is to tear yourself apart daily, inch by inch. Living like this, you cannot even enjoy the top skim of life, for you constantly waver beneath what is deepest and what is most false. And you never find your way home.

But even to this torn person God keeps reaching out. He keeps loving and wanting. It is almost as if the deep and smothered stream of joy in that wavering person cries out to heaven for refreshing, and God tries with all the power of His Holy Spirit to break through the dam of youth's false decisions, his false grabs for the false goddesses.

Whatever the case, there is no stopping the false claims on the young soul. Walk out of the Los Angeles air terminal and you see the Cadillacs lining the curb. You hear the money jingled out loud so that you catch the sound of it and know what makes Hollywood tick. Or wander into a divorce court and listen to the reasons why young marrieds cut apart from each other, give up their children, and live alone or in adultery. Then you know how loud the false calls have become. And you may know also how that river of joy inside any Christians among these people is drying up.

All this is agony beyond any illness. For though the whirlwind of the Gospel cannot be penned, cannot be predicted, it remains the only lasting joy of the soul.

To know that you are loved, that you are loved eternally! To know that you are called to every morning and every night, and to feel the joy rising in you to meet the call, and to live with an enlivening hope raising you up every time you think you cannot go another step! To know that everything happening to you — your school life, your social life, your disappointments, your successes, your failures — has an answer in this Gospel of Jesus Christ calling to you!

That is resurrection. That is the reviving of the waters.

Just to know it *can* happen to you is joy.

Say It for Your Lord

Our Lord Jesus Christ is *the Word of God* in human form. Everything we know from the time He walked the earth in full sight of people has come to us in the form of words.

Words carry the dignity and touch of our Lord Himself. He chose them to be the revealers of Himself to us. They are all tied up with Him and His Gospel. When you talk Jesus Christ, you want to talk in words as well as in life.

The worst happens when high school Christians lose their longing to give words to their Lord. Then the plan of God for youth's outreach to youth no longer reaches out. Our life purpose dries up like a puddle in the desert. Our own selves grow inward like sores that are not touched by the sun. When words die, people die inside, inch by inch.

Yet that's what people are doing in the strange dearth of life-giving words that has fixed into a death mask many a high school, community, and congregation. Young persons themselves can see each other fifty-two Sundays in the year and never mention the name of Jesus Christ in personal conversation. The Gospel has gone professional. Why mention Christ when that's precisely the preacher's job? I'm no good at words, you know. That's up to the Reverend.

But it isn't up to "the Reverend" alone.

Your whole personality lives because the Holy Spirit lives in you.

Your own Lord Jesus Christ sent Him. This Holy Spirit lives in you under God's own orders. He lives in you to comfort you, strengthen you, enrich you, fill you with His special life. *And* to talk through you!

What does this make you?

Priceless.

Priceless to the Lord, because He owns you.

Priceless to people, because the Holy Spirit is reaching out to *them* through you.

Priceless because the work of just going on talking simply has to be done, even when it has to be done by young people who —

a) would rather be doing something else;
b) are tired of talking, talking, talking;
c) are tired of "the church," "religion," "people."

Even when you *are* really tired, the Holy Spirit lives in you. Even then He thrives in you, wants to use you to get His love and power out to those people He has led into your life.

"Say it!" sounds like a glib pitchman's motto. But it's a thousand times tougher than anything like that. It's talking your salvation when you would rather sit on a beach and growl at the world. It's yearning to love people when you find yourself hating them. It's longing to feel your own heart melt inside you at the sight of a face hungry for light.

You are the person made priceless for this loving labor. Nobody else can touch the ones you can touch in your own particular way in this one particular time of your life. God has loved you — for a purpose far beyond you.

The purpose is words, talk, communication — all of it to other priceless ones. To others, boys and girls, men and women, called in the eternal driving and loving purpose of the Holy Spirit.

Say it: "He loves me, He loves me all the way."

Now think: *There are others waiting to hear just this.*

They have to hear it — to live.

Will Christian Youth Survive?

Thinking together about Jesus Christ and growing in His life may seem just a little silly if Moscow or Peking lets loose the hell cooped up like a lion in a too-small cage. There's the big H — the hydrogen warhead — and if that won't do the trick, well, you can move on to the real deadly stuff: the germs, the cobalt that could kill everything everywhere, the nerve gas.

As we said, in the face of all this, reminding ourselves of the love of God can bore to tears. What does the love of God mean — what *can* it mean — when the hate of man can liquefy any one of us at any instant? Talk about Christian youth! By the time this gets into print, there may not *be* any Christian youth!

So why waste our breath?

There's a queer kind of logic in all this. It makes sense in a horrible, sad way. Not divine sense, but human sense. Human sense can get all set to throw in the towel over the caged-up death in Moscow or Washington! Human sense, maybe even common sense, can answer to the whole ghastly mess: "We've had it. That's all. We've had it."

Not divine sense, though. Not that. Nowhere

in all the Gospel of Jesus Christ, nowhere in any part of His Scripture would you find the tossing of a towel because the world has got so tough — too tough to live in, too tough to face, too tough to do anything about.

Instead you find that unbelievable "I have overcome the world." That from Christ. Or from Paul: "I can do all things through Christ, who strengthens me." Of all the nerve — that in a world dominated by the Roman picked soldiers!

Yet it's true. That's divine sense.

Man is still the image of God — not the Bomb. And into this feeble, fumbling skin and bones God still breathes Himself. For this skin and bones He still gives Himself, just as once for all He gave Himself into dying and the living death of daily living amid the hatreds and the fears of Palestine, zero A. D.

You tell me that this man, this youth into whom God has breathed Himself, cannot finally do more in the world and *with* the world than we have ever dreamed.

I say he can. I say she can.

One regret is that no such Christian sits on the throne in Peking or in the Kremlin in Moscow or in most of the countries of the world. So we Christians keep wondering about the heart and the hand of the man without God. How can you expect anything but the worst from this situation?

But even the man without God lives only because God lets him live. It's one thing to talk about the love of God. It's another thing to talk about His power. Such a power it is that God can sit in the heavens and laugh. The bomb blasts can only tickle His sense of humor, so pitiful they are compared with the power He keeps in His little finger — the power to shape the whole earth and the whole universe that swirls in space and every single fiber of life and resurrection and death within this mass.

All these words don't touch the God of power. Just as nothing can describe the fullness, the warmth, the thundering sea of His love.

But all of it is divine sense.

If we survive, it will be because He wants us to go on living Him, talking Him, reminding ourselves of Him. And if we do not survive, it won't be because He couldn't control Moscow and Peking. It will be because Moscow and Peking are helping Him to carry out His will.

It will be because Moscow and Peking are helping Him to bring us, all together, person-to-Person with our Lord of love and power.

Will you survive? Believe me, no bomb can really touch you either. Just as no bomb can touch the love and power of God in Jesus Christ. For you are altogether with Him — here or there.

You will survive. His love has made you alive with a life that rises above youth or middle age or old age or Moscow or cobalt or the worst that man can do to man.

You are the apple of God's eye. You are part of His body on earth. He loves you with a love beyond time.

He loves you with everything He is.

That means more than any news headline you'll ever see.

The Meaning of Our Burden

Can any young Christian understand how the Lord actually keeps on loving by sending an extra-heavy burden to live with — and maybe to die with?

I can't understand it — not after years of being a minister of Jesus Christ. I see it happen all right. I see people actually getting stronger and getting happier — in the deepest sort of way — while they struggle under a torturing cross.

Whatever miracle is going on here, it goes on also in the lives of Christian youth. These heartaches of adolescence, these broken loves and shattered hopes, are sent by our Lord no less than other burdens. Our struggle with our bodies, our minds, our spirits — our longing to see some divine purpose shape and guide our lives in spite of all the impulses that pull us this way and that — can build us as well as tear us down.

I don't know why, exactly. I don't know *how*, certainly. But I do know that this process belongs to the chemistry of our Lord. I do know that it happens.

I am only a preacher of the Gospel of Jesus Christ. This is all I have ever been, and I don't think it likely that I could really be anything else. Yet even in this single calling, which to many people sounds so ideally peaceful, I have come to know a burden. I have come to learn just a little of what it is to wear the yoke of Jesus Christ.

So far as I can see, there is no occupation or calling free from such a burden. Every young minister in my graduating class at the seminary had stars in his eyes on diploma day I think we all envisioned morning devotions in some white parsonage study, our prayers touched by nothing more from the outside world than the ticking of some aged clock in the study corner. We held before us the faces of steady, dedicated people who would stand by our ministry. We thought of eyes lighting at the preaching of the Gospel we had pored over in the Gothic classrooms. There seemed then to be *no burden at all* in the ministry of this Gospel.

But the real facts of the ministry and the church slapped me in the face like a slab of ice. The whirling swirl of committee and mimeograph, the walking of hot dust and gravel for a full summer to find one person willing to risk a visit to the church, the preaching to empty pews on a summer morning, the battle for sanity waged by my members working on automobile assembly lines — all this added up to a burden which simply had to be carried in the name of Jesus Christ.

Even to a preacher, burdens seem pesky. But they make a person grow. They drive you to prayer — that longing where you seem so small to yourself, so tall to your Lord. They drive you to remember the One who died all for you — because that is the last great fact to keep you going, and you know it.

Maybe this is the final meaning to every Christian youth's burden. Maybe burdens not only preach the Gospel — they push you *into* the Gospel. They put one hand on the small of your back, another on your shoulder, and walk you with painful pressure right back to Jesus Christ.

That's expensive transportation — and sometimes terribly heart-aching going.

But it gets you there. And if it didn't, your life wouldn't be worth a smile or a tear. Which would add up to about the dullest life you ever lived.

This Name, This Person, This Glory

There is no other name to give joy like this.

Everything solid inside us is answer to this name and this Person.

We smile at our boy or girl friend. We think, *This person is my happiness.*

But without the answer of Jesus Christ deep, deep in us — deep beyond our knowing sometimes — looking at our own best friend would be disheartening. Perhaps even, in a morning when things went wrong, completely saddening. After all, what can mean anything at all, if Jesus Christ is dead?

Or we go to a football game on an October afternoon, relishing the fusion of color and coffee and the surge of a thousand high school people sensing a oneness with one another in all of the splash of autumn red. "This is great, just great!" But what is great is the *souls* of these people — souls who can live and feel this oneness and this richness of Jesus Christ.

Without the awareness of having been once met by the Christ who has conquered time, we could not so easily enjoy even a game of checkers. His presence mightily changes all of our life, but the changes He makes go so deep that they do not always send up shock waves to our consciousness. We cannot count on knowing what is happening to us. We can only believe that what is happening to us is happening because Jesus Christ is.

So our enjoyment of Jesus Christ, our answer to Him from the depths of us, flares out into every field of our personalities and lives.

He is, and He is the One that calls from us the answer that makes living through these high school years not just bearable but victorious!

There are a lot of things to win victories over in the high school years. Flaws and scars in our own personalities come to light then — as well as the failures in other people whom we once adored without question. Strong pulls and stronger desires tearing us inside, leading us toward outcomes we fear. For the first time we see how far short we are going to fall behind any ideal goal we have set for ourselves.

We will not conquer all of these. Maybe none of them!

But the name of Jesus Christ will itself *be* our victory. Even where we fail, even when we fail — even then and there the name and the person of Jesus Christ will stay with us.

So dying we can live. So failing we can find victory. So fearing we can find forgiveness.

Jesus Christ. That name, that Person, *is* our glory.

Now we can try to change lives.

Because we have a glory.

Prayers to Help You Live

In Thanks for My Faith

My Lord Jesus Christ, I come to Your altar with no sense of pride. I know it is my parents who led me there — my people, my fellow church members, my friends.

I know that without these people You gave me, there might not be faith in me. There might have been no Baptism. There might have been no life of You in me at all.

So I thank You for these my people, my Christian people. I thank You for sending them to me, for leading them to be a light and a guide to my road. I thank You for the warm, surrounding sense of Your presence. I thank You for all the rich moments of my faith and for the promise of richer joys at Your Supper.

I thank You, my own personal Redeemer, for Yourself.

Before Communion

Savior, today You are giving me more of Yourself than ever before, Your very own body and blood.

When You first shared this holy sacrament with Your disciples, did You think of me as a disciple also? For I truly want to be one and sincerely want to live as real a disciple's life as Your first followers did in Galilee.

I know how hard it is to try to live like that to-day, in the kind of world this has grown to be. Nothing is easy today, my Lord, not even for a young person. So I know how much I'm asking for when I ask for the strength and the love and the peace to live as Your disciple.

Please let Your sacrament act as a strength-giving renewing of my life with You. Let Your body and Your blood surge into me and knit me closer with You, so that my faith mounts into a thriving energy.

So that I may be more Your disciple — right here today, my Lord.

For Knowing Myself in Him

It is only in You, my Lord Jesus Christ, that I can ever really see myself as I am.

It is only in You that I can accept myself for what I am.

For You have covered me over with Your own righteousness. You have surrounded me with Your salvation. In Your presence I know myself to be a child of my Father in heaven — no matter what my inward state. No matter what I know myself to be like in my worse moments.

Here, then, my Savior, I thank You for placing Your righteousness upon me through Your dying and Your rising again. Wholly and gratefully I accept Your righteousness as my only righteousness. Wholly and gratefully I admit myself to have no merit but what You have gained for me.

In that light, beautiful and perfect Savior, I accept myself also as a forgiven person — one who can never have perfection but one who can always count on having You. Teach me the art of accepting myself under You, my Lord, and drive off from me the snares of pride and ambition that would turn my life into a self-seeking thing.

Only let we know You. Only let me rejoice in Your righteousness. Only let me forever dwell in the shadow of Your wing and in the certainty of Your redemption.

My Lord, blessings and praise be to You forever.

When I Am Too Conscious of Myself

My Savior, only in remembering Your perfection can I find any peace at all.

I know this best when I try hardest to find some high promise within myself. Exactly then I always grow most unhappy with everyone else — and with all of life around me. To search inside myself is only to see how terribly and how really I need You, Your church, Your Gospel, Your sacraments, Your constant nourishing love!

But knowing this cannot free me from myself, my Lord. I still look too much inward. I still find myself bounded on all four sides by myself. I still often choose to stay within those four walls rather than to cast my eyes upward toward You, upward to the hills, from where my only help can come.

So here I ask You, Savior, to free me from myself. I ask You to pull me loose from the four walls that hold me inside the prison of my own person. Instead let me think of *Your* person, Your work, Your life and death and resurrection for me and all my fellow believers in You.

Free me with Your love, Redeemer. Free me to move outside myself in love for You and Yours.

In a Time of New Friendships

Thanks, my Lord, for the new people You have sent into my life. Thanks especially for the fellowship of those whose faith feeds my faith in the company of all Christians.

Most of all, my Savior, thank You for Your constant and warming friendship. For living within me, for surrounding me, for filling the universe with Your power and glory, I thank You.

Certainly the friends You have given me are mirrors of Your love and Your friendship.

Surely then that different kind of friendship that

grows between girl and boy can mirror Your kind of love, Your kind of care. I know this is the kind of relationship I want to find with every friend, whether girl or boy.

For this I pray You, my greatest Friend of all.

For the spirit to reflect Your love in the face that I turn to my friends.

For the love to see in the faces of my friends the mirrored reflection of Your own love for me.

For the purity to see my friendships so and to keep them just so — in Your image, my Savior and my Lord.

When I Have Lost Sight of You

O loving Redeemer, what can I offer in prayer when for so long a time I have forgotten You?

The joys of my church have faded. I find little rejoicing in my worship. I speak Your name with small excitement. Dull inside and out, I would like to do anything else but sing Your praise.

Yet deep within me, my Lord and my King, I hold an allegiance to You which runs far beyond feelings. I sense a desire for You which moves much richer and swifter than a hidden mountain stream. Although on the surface of my life and my person I may seem dead to Your joys, yet beneath the flow of my outer self there is the sure longing for Your presence and Your grace which only You can answer.

That is what I ask for now — Your answer. Your answer in spite of my coldness. Your response in spite of my outer dullness. Your tenderest reply to that deepest cry of my spirit in spite of the outside tiredness and boredom which I may show to my fellow Christians.

Remember me, my Savior, in those moments when because of my humanness I cannot remember You. Love me when I cannot show love to You. Enliven my senses to Your glory, and quicken me to Your everlasting presence with me.

O faithful Lord, stay faithful when I am most unfaithful and most unworthy. Even as I believe You are so faithful, so I pledge to You my deep love when my shallow life can show it least.

I love You, my Lord God. I love You, Jesus Christ, my Life and my Light.

When Nothing Is Going Right

Lord, I am humbled by my constant failures at so many things I try to do.

Every day I learn how limited I really am — even in trying to serve You! Sometimes nothing I do turns out right, even when I think straight and work hardest.

It's then I wonder most how You can ever use someone like me in Your kingdom.

My Savior, is there any use for a person like me — so loaded down with failure and with self-wonder? Can You really build Your church with human beings as frail and faulty as I?

Yet I know that's what Your Word does say — even though I find it so hard to believe when I come to thinking about *me*. I do know that the disciples had their failings too. I do know that there's not a perfect person living in the pages of all Scripture but You Yourself. So the church — my church — must have been built on humans with human failings!

Yet, my Savior, somehow all this knowing has to come into me, has to live in me. Or I will never have any hope in myself. Even though I know You, I will never believe that You could use me — unless You lead me straight into this faith.

So lead me, loving Lord.

So help me not only to understand You but to understand *me*.

Help me to understand myself under You, with You, in You, and You in me.

And if I cannot understand it, my Lord, just help me to believe it — and so to believe a little in myself.

Before Church Worship

Lord, there is a light to Your face that nothing in the world can equal. There is a peace to Your being that no human being can touch. There is a soft stillness in Your church that no man-made silence can meet.

Now when I am ready to be filled again with this miracle of worship, I pray You to rekindle in me that first delight and amazement of my confirmation day, to light again the flame in me that You have lighted before in this place I love with this people I love.

I pray You to build a chapel in my heart.

I pray You to live in it, to warm it, to make it sing like the church where I am going today.

So may I be Your chapel, and my church be a living force in me.

For One Most Loved

O Beauty of my dearest friend, You alone can shape the wonder of a human soul.

You alone create the beauty of a beautiful girl or the strength of a strong young man.

You alone can bring Your people to meet. You alone can cause our eyes to see each other with love, our hearts to care for each other with concern, and our desires to rise up only for the good of the other.

I pray You now, as never before, to shape my desire as Yours is formed. I pray You to make my love purely for the joy of the one I love. I pray You to keep away from me the lust of selfishness, of self-satisfaction, of self-drive and self-wishing.

Instead lead me to long only for the good of the one I love. And lead my love to be good, as Yours is good. Lead my love to be upbuilding, not destructive. Purifying, not terrifying. Clean and clear as a waterfall and never an injury to anyone.

I pray for the one I love, my Lord and my Savior. And I pray for the love with which I love, that it may be like Yours: self-giving and with a self that is worth giving.

With a self that is loved by You and knows it.

On a Rainy Day

My own Lord, when my spirits fade into deep gray, be my returning Joy.

When I cannot find any happiness in life, be Life renewing and refreshing in me.

My Lord and my God, I am not able of myself to brush off the despair and night that the world thrusts at me. I am not able to drive off the worries and doubts that life on this planet must bring.

I am only able to ask You to hold me up, to act as my Strength and my Life, to fill my spirit with a rich warmness and a steady desire for You.

That even the rainiest day can become one of communion with You — that even the grayest clouds can increase our life with each other — only this I can ask. And so I can leave my burden of sadness with You and carry away with me only a longing and a hunger.

Fill my longing and my hunger, my Lord. But let me not stop longing and hungering, even as You will not stop filling me with the happiness of Yourself.

For Your Spirit and Life

Savior, breathe into me the breath of life.

I want nothing more than to live by Your Spirit. I want to love. I want to love out of the certainty that I am loved. I want to carry out the work You have put before me to do. I want to live with that sense of purpose which only Your love and Your calling can give me.

I want to live You.

No one knows more than I do how far from this kind of life I am. No one feels the pain of being so far away more than I do. Yet I know You share this suffering. I know You bear this cross too.

So, Savior, I can be bold in coming to You for the gift of Your Spirit. I ask You for Yourself. I cry out for Yourself. For only through Yourself can I live at all. Without You I perish. Without You there simply is no life.

Come into me, Life. Fill me, Spirit. Live, and drive me into living, loving, being Yours and Your people's person.

In longing for this, I rest my life with You.